LET'S MAKE ART

SCRAP PAPER ART

SUSIE BROOKS

PowerKiDS
press

Published in 2018 by **The Rosen Publishing Group, Inc.**
29 East 21st Street, New York, NY 10010

Cataloging-in-Publication Data
Names: Brooks, Susie.
Title: Scrap paper art / Susie Brooks.
Description: New York : PowerKids Press, 2018. | Series: Let's make art | Includes index.
Identifiers: ISBN 9781538323205 (pbk.) | ISBN 9781538322253 (library bound) |
    ISBN 9781538323212 (6 pack)
Subjects: LCSH: Paper work--Juvenile literature. | Handicraft--Juvenile literature.
Classification: LCC TT870.B76 2018 | DDC 745.54--dc23

Editor: Elizabeth Brent
Design: nicandlou

Manufactured in China
CPSIA Compliance Information: Batch BW18PK: For Further Information contact
Rosen Publishing, New York, New York at 1-800-237-9932.

CONTENTS

LET'S MAKE ART!

How often do you recycle food packaging, wrapping paper, or magazines? Next time, stop and look! Scrap paper and cardboard is perfect for making all sorts of artwork, as you'll find out in this book.

WHAT YOU NEED

If you like a picture in a magazine, cut it out and save it! Even black-and-white newspaper can be turned into beautiful designs. You can use the backs of old envelopes or cardboard boxes as the background for your pictures. Ribbons, cupcake wrappers, and doilies are great for extra bits of decoration.

FOR THE PROJECTS IN THIS BOOK, IT ALSO HELPS TO HAVE A FEW BASIC ART SUPPLIES:
- ✓ A PENCIL AND ERASER
- ✓ SCISSORS
- ✓ GLUE
- ✓ PLAIN WHITE PAPER OR CARD STOCK
- ✓ COLORED PAPER OR CARD STOCK, INCLUDING BLACK
- ✓ COLORED PENCILS
- ✓ MARKERS
- ✓ CRAYONS
- ✓ A RULER
- ✓ A HOLE PUNCH
- ✓ DOUBLE-SIDED TAPE
- ✓ A SPONGE

HANDY HINTS

Before you start, lay down plenty of newspaper to protect the surface you're working on.

To pick up tiny bits of paper like the circles from a hole punch, lick your finger and the paper will cling to it.

Work at a size you feel comfortable with — if something's too tiny to cut, try doing it bigger.

Save scraps of paper that you've cut away — they'll be useful another time!

Nail clippers are handy for cutting small paper shapes. Some craft scissors have a special zig-zag blade for fancy edges.

If you don't have paper in the color you want, you can always paint your own.

There are templates on pages 30-31 to help you draw some useful shapes, but don't try to copy everything exactly. Half the fun is testing ideas of your own!

When you see this LOGO, you might want to ask an adult to help.

BATTY SILHOUETTES

USE COLORED TISSUE PAPER TO MAKE THESE BATTY BACKGROUNDS.

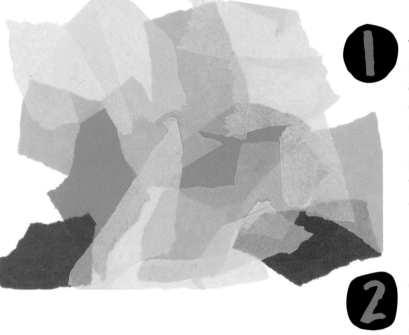

1 Tear up scraps of tissue paper and glue them to a sheet of white paper or card stock. Keep going until the paper is covered. Don't worry if you only have one or two colors. You can overlap the pieces to create different shades.

2 When your paper is full, draw around a mug, glass, or roll of tape and cut out several circles.

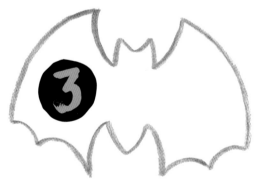

3

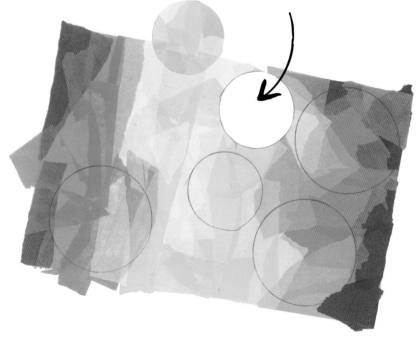

Now practice drawing bat shapes like this one. Make them small enough to fit inside your tissue paper circles. Copy them onto black paper and cut them out. There are some templates on p. 30 to help you.

4 Now practice drawing bat shapes like these. Make them small enough to fit inside your tissue paper circles. Copy them onto black paper and cut them out. There are some templates on p. 30 to help you out!

5 Glue a bat to each circle. Then, arrange them on a sheet of black paper and glue them down.

MAKE A BLACK CAT OR AN OWL TO GO WITH YOUR BATS!

FANCY FLOWERS

TRANSFORM OLD SCRAPS OF WRAPPING PAPER, WALLPAPER, AND OTHER PATTERNED PAPER INTO A COLORFUL VASE OF FLOWERS.

HERE ARE A FEW WAYS TO MAKE YOUR FLOWERS:

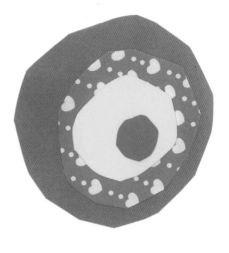

1 Cut out rough, circular shapes from different colored papers and glue smaller ones on top of the larger ones.

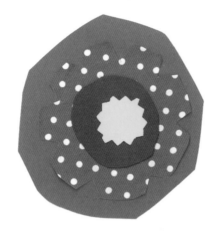

2 Cut out petal shapes and arrange them in a flower design, like this.

3 Overlap some large round shapes in a circle, then stick a smaller one in the middle.

4 Cut out eight narrow strips of paper, all the same length. Glue two in a cross shape, then add the others one by one, like the spokes of a wheel. Glue a different colored circle in the middle.

TIP

YOU COULD FOLD A SHEET OF CARD STOCK IN HALF TO MAKE A CARD AND GLUE YOUR FLOWERS ON THE FRONT!

YOU CAN EXPERIMENT BY CUTTING AND LAYERING DIFFERENT SHAPES OF PAPER.

5 Cut some stalks and leaves from green paper and glue your bright bouquet of flowers onto a sheet of white paper. Finish with a vase shape in any color you like.

DANGLY DRAGONS

Use scraps of colored cardboard or packaging to make these friendly fire-breathers.

These little circles of paper came out of a hole punch.

1 Cut out a triangle for the head, about 2 inches (5 cm) wide at the top. There's a template on p. 30 if you need it.

2 Glue the triangle onto a piece of scrap paper, then glue on smaller shapes, like these, to create a face. Cut the whole thing out.

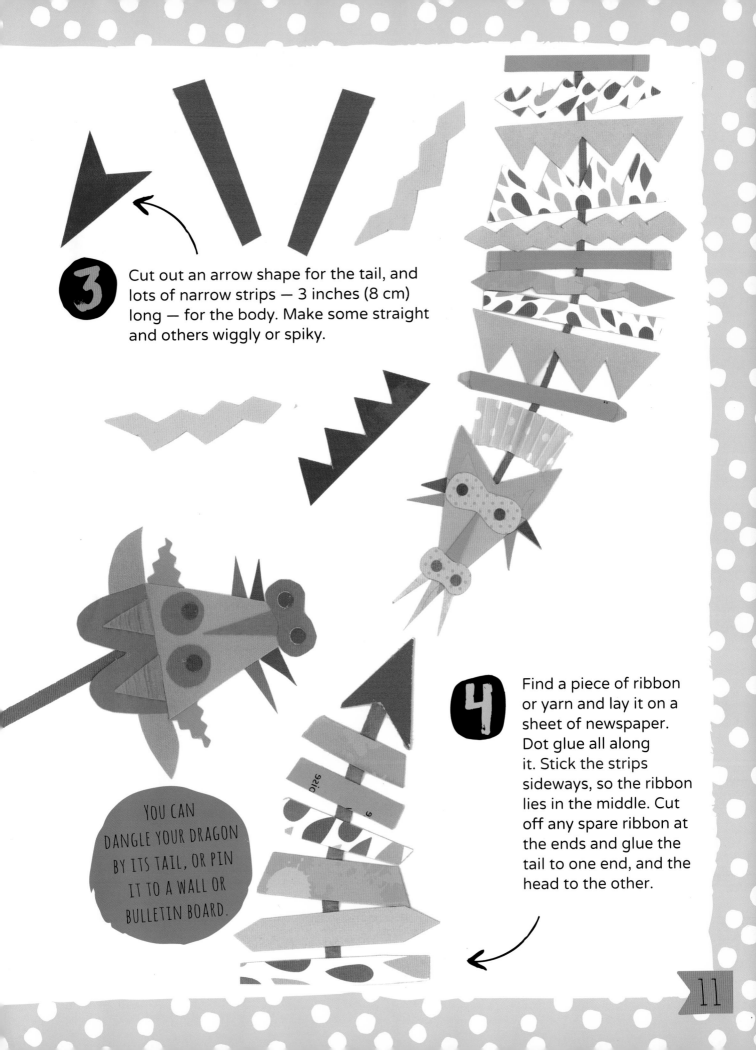

3 Cut out an arrow shape for the tail, and lots of narrow strips — 3 inches (8 cm) long — for the body. Make some straight and others wiggly or spiky.

4 Find a piece of ribbon or yarn and lay it on a sheet of newspaper. Dot glue all along it. Stick the strips sideways, so the ribbon lies in the middle. Cut off any spare ribbon at the ends and glue the tail to one end, and the head to the other.

YOU CAN DANGLE YOUR DRAGON BY ITS TAIL, OR PIN IT TO A WALL OR BULLETIN BOARD.

SWIRLY SNAIL

WRAPPING PAPER AND WALLPAPER SCRAPS WORK WELL FOR THIS SMILEY SNAIL.

1 Roughly cut out a circle from solid-colored paper, about the size of a small plate or bowl. This will be the background for the snail's shell.

2 Using bits of patterned paper, cut out lots of pointy triangle shapes to fit in the circle, like this.

A BLACK-AND-WHITE SNAIL MADE FROM NEWSPAPER IS FUN TO DO, TOO.

3 Arrange the triangles with the points in the middle of the circle, and glue them down.

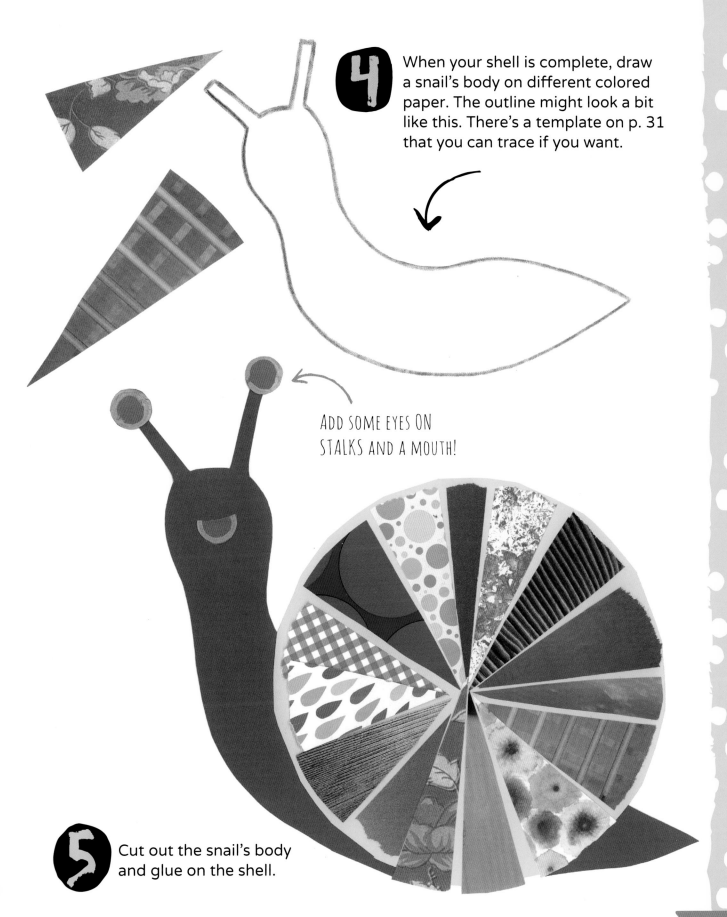

4 When your shell is complete, draw a snail's body on different colored paper. The outline might look a bit like this. There's a template on p. 31 that you can trace if you want.

ADD SOME EYES ON STALKS AND A MOUTH!

5 Cut out the snail's body and glue on the shell.

BIRDS IN BOOTS

Create a FLOCK of birds wearing colorful rubber boots!

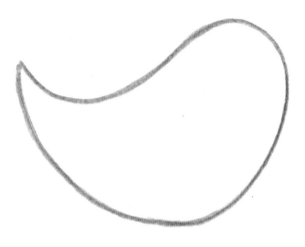

1 Practice drawing bird shapes like these, with a rounded head and a pointed tail. Draw some onto scrap paper and cut them out.

WHY NOT TRY MAKING A HEN, A DUCK, OR A PARROT?

2 Glue your bird shapes onto white paper and draw around them. Cut out wing and beak shapes, and glue them on. Draw two legs and an eye.

YOU COULD ADD SOME SWIRLY TAIL FEATHERS.

3 Cut out some boot shapes from spare wrapping paper or wallpaper, or paint your own patterns.

NOW DRESS UP YOUR BIRDS IN SOME BOOTS!

4 Glue the boots over the ends of your birds' legs.

THIS PAPER TOWEL MAKES A GREAT PUDDLE.

FRUITY PATTERN

A FEW SIMPLE SHAPES CAN MAKE A PRETTY PATTERN!

1 You'll need a selection of paper squares, all the same size, in a few different colors. One way to make these is to cut strips 2 inches (5 cm) wide from a sheet of paper, then mark every 2 inches (5 cm) along the strip and cut into squares.

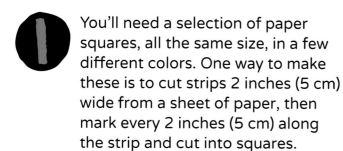

2 On each square, draw a simple fruit shape. The stalk of the fruit should come right to one edge of the square.

LEAVES CAN BE TRICKY TO CUT, SO LEAVE THEM OUT IF YOU WANT TO MAKE IT EASIER.

3 Carefully cut all around the fruit, starting from the stalk. Keep both the inside and the outside piece whole. When you've cut out one piece of fruit, you can draw around it on a different colored square!

4 Arrange your fruit shapes on a big sheet of dark-colored paper. Put an outside piece next to an inside piece, and so on. Build up a colorful block. Try putting some pieces upside down or sideways.

WHEN YOU'RE HAPPY WITH YOUR DESIGN, GLUE THE PIECES DOWN. YOU COULD DISPLAY THE PICTURE IN YOUR KITCHEN.

NOSY BOOKMARKS

CARDBOARD MAKES A GREAT BASE FOR THESE NOSY ANIMALS. SLOT THEM OVER A PAGE IN YOUR BOOK, WITH THE NOSE PEERING DOWN TO MARK YOUR PLACE.

1 Think of an animal with a long nose or snout and draw the outline of its head onto card stock.

AN ELEPHANT MIGHT LOOK LIKE THIS!

RECTANGLE

SMALL ARCH

2 Cut out the head shape, then cut a rectangle for the body with a small arch between the legs, like this.

3 Tear up colored pieces from a newspaper or magazine and glue them all over your animal.

DRAW A FACE ON YOUR ANIMAL.

TIP
Try making some different nosy animals, such as this giraffe! There are templates on p.30 if you need.

Tuck your book page under here.

4 When it's covered, stick a strip of double-sided sticky tape along the top of the body. Stick the top of the head onto the tape. The bottom of the head and the nose should not be stuck down.

SHADY TREES

You don't need BRIGHTLY colored paper to create an eye-catching picture!

Cut a strip of a brown paper bag. Make the edges a bit wobbly, like a tree trunk. Glue it onto a white background.

Add shorter, thinner strips for branches. Cut leaf shapes from old newspaper and glue them on.

Now cut a narrower strip from light brown cardboard, the same height as your tree trunk. Glue this down on one side of the trunk to give the effect of light shining on it.

TRY CUTTING OUT OR DRAWING SOME ANIMALS TO HIDE AMONG YOUR TREES. THE DARK COLORS HERE WERE CUT OUT FROM OLD MAGAZINES.

TIP

IF YOU MAKE A TREE THE WHOLE HEIGHT OF YOUR PAPER, IT WILL SEEM CLOSER THAN THE OTHERS.

4 You can create a shadow on the ground by cutting a strip of brown paper the width of the tree trunk and gluing it at an angle at the bottom of your tree trunk.

21

PUPS IN PRINT

SIMPLE TORN-UP NEWSPAPER IS PERFECT FOR THESE PUPS.

1 Tear a big shape for the body and a smaller one for the head. Glue them to some plain paper.

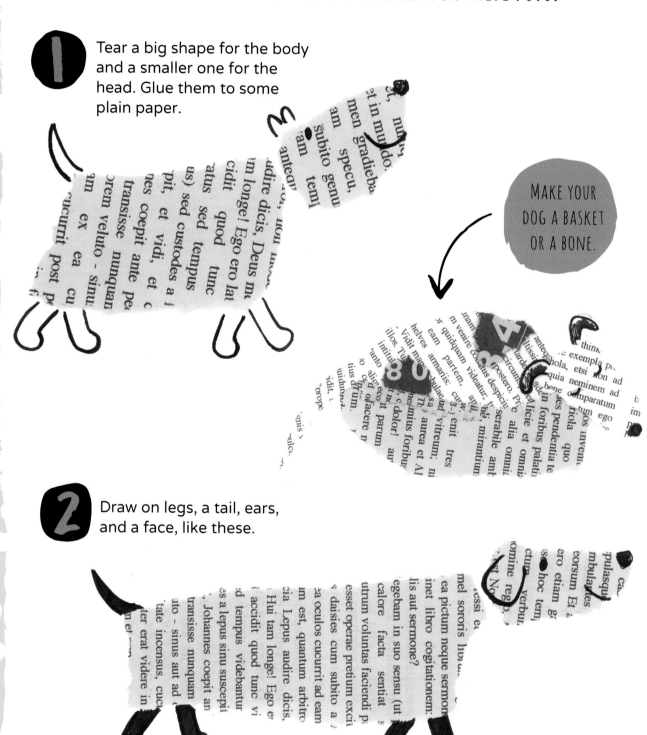

MAKE YOUR DOG A BASKET OR A BONE.

2 Draw on legs, a tail, ears, and a face, like these.

3 To make a shaggy dog, draw an outline of the animal in pencil. There are some templates on p. 31 to help. Then tear up lots of thin strips of newspaper. Glue the top of each strip to the top of the dog and let the rest hang down.

CUT OUT CLOUD SHAPES FOR A FLUFFY POODLE.

. . . OR A COLLAR!

PEOPLE PYRAMID

YOU CAN HAVE LOTS OF FUN WITH SIMPLE COLLAGE FIGURES. GLUE THEM ONTO A PIECE OF WHITE PAPER OR CARD STOCK.

1 Cut out some head shapes from scrap paper or magazines. Draw or glue on different faces. Try using lips or ears from a photo! Punch some holes in paper with a hole punch and use the little circles for eyes or cheeks.

2 Look for patterned paper and try cutting these simple shapes for clothes. You might find fabric textures in a catalogue. Cut strips for arms and legs, and two oval feet.

CUT OUT HAIR FROM PHOTOS!

3 When you've practiced making people, try piling some up in a pyramid shape! Start with the bottom row, and then perch the others on top.

CUT UP A PAPER DOILY FOR FRILLY CLOTHES.

YOU COULD ADD SOME PARTY HATS AND BOWS. THIS TUTU IS MADE FROM A CUPCAKE WRAPPER!

FLIGHTY KITES

MIX AND MATCH DIFFERENT PAPERS FOR A FLURRY OF KITES FLYING HIGH!

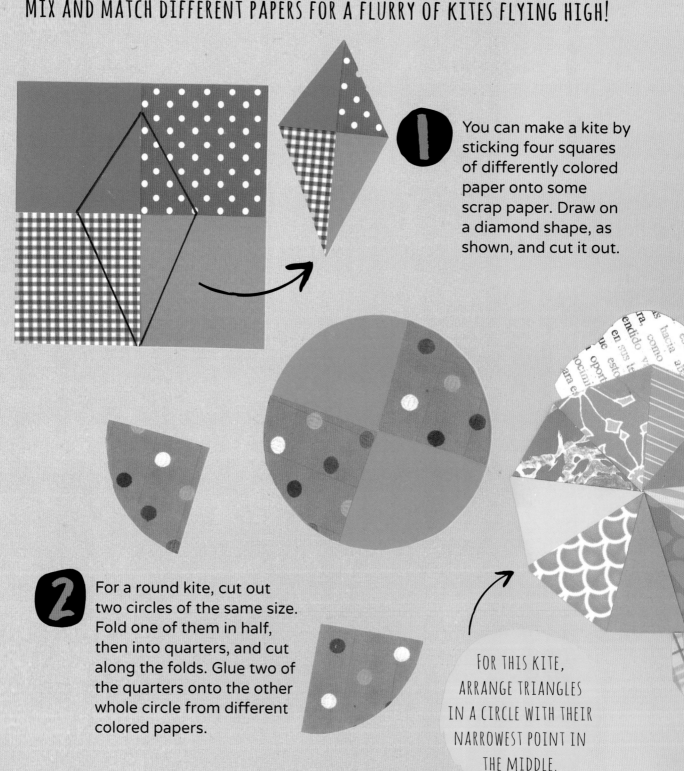

1 You can make a kite by sticking four squares of differently colored paper onto some scrap paper. Draw on a diamond shape, as shown, and cut it out.

2 For a round kite, cut out two circles of the same size. Fold one of them in half, then into quarters, and cut along the folds. Glue two of the quarters onto the other whole circle from different colored papers.

FOR THIS KITE, ARRANGE TRIANGLES IN A CIRCLE WITH THEIR NARROWEST POINT IN THE MIDDLE.

Cut out cloud shapes from old newspaper and scribble over them with white crayon or paint.

Add some colorful flowing tails to your kites using strips or triangles of paper.

3 Glue everything onto a piece of pale blue paper.

WOVEN WALLS

WEAVE WINDOWS INTO SOME PAPERY CITY WALLS!

1 Cut a sheet of paper in half lengthwise, and then fold it half lengthwise. Mark lines across from the folded edge, spacing them about 1 inch (3 cm) apart. Stop each line about 0.5 inches (1 cm) from the opposite edge. Cut along the lines and open the paper out.

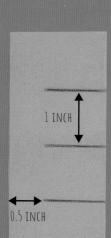

1 INCH

0.5 INCH

WEAVE THESE IN AND OUT THROUGH THE SLITS.

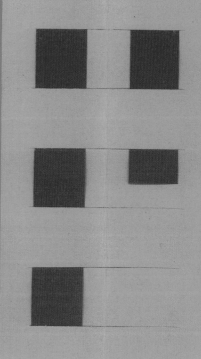

2

From a different color of paper, cut out some strips the same height as your rectangle and about 1 inch (3 cm) wide.

TEMPLATES

BATS
P. 6–7

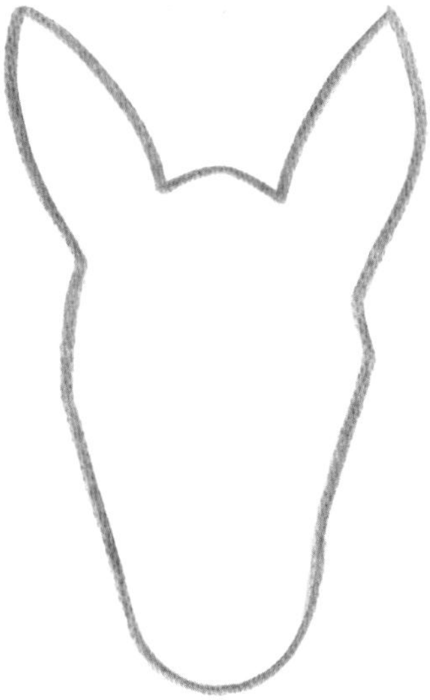

DRAGON'S
FACE
P. 10–11

ZEBRA AND
GIRAFFE
P. 18–19

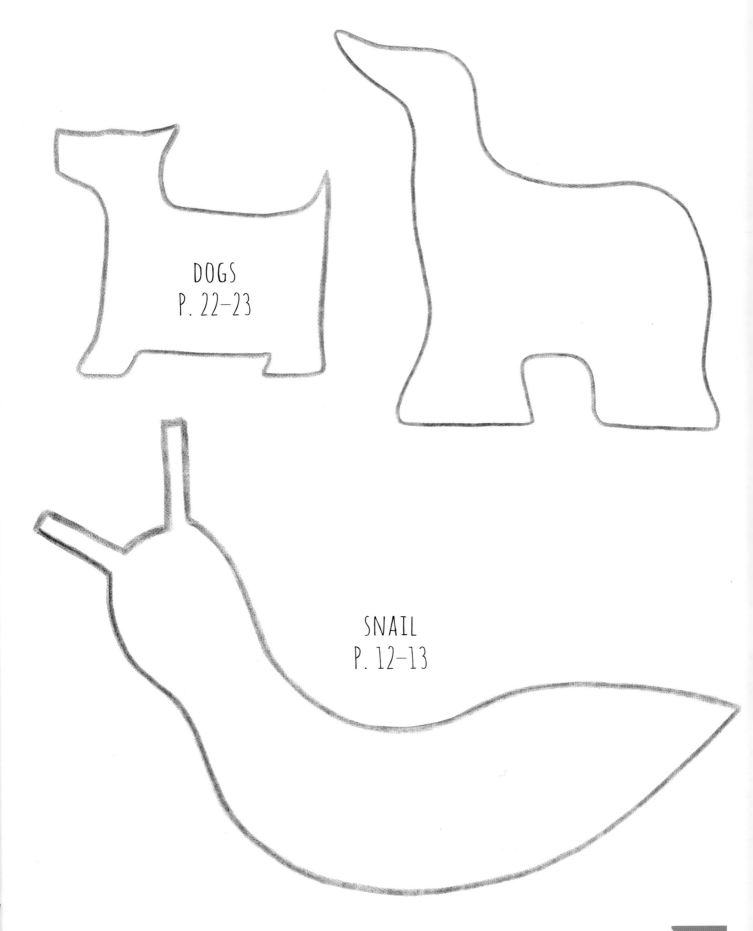

DOGS
P. 22–23

SNAIL
P. 12–13

GLOSSARY

COLLAGE: ART MADE BY STICKING PIECES OF PAPER, FABRIC, OR OTHER MATERIALS ONTO A SURFACE

CORRUGATED: RIDGED, LIKE THE INSIDE LAYER OF SOME CARDBOARD

LAYERING: ARRANGING PIECES ON TOP OF ONE ANOTHER

OVERLAP: TO PARTLY COVER ONE SHAPE WITH ANOTHER

SILHOUETTE: A PLAIN DARK SHAPE, USUALLY SHOWN AGAINST A LIGHT OR COLORED BACKGROUND

WEAVE: TO COMBINE THREADS OR STRIPS OF PAPER AT RIGHT ANGLES TO ONE ANOTHER BY PASSING THEM OVER AND UNDER

TEMPLATE: A SHAPE USED AS A GUIDELINE TO TRACE

TEXTURE: THE FEEL OR APPEARANCE OF A SURFACE, SUCH AS FLUFFY WOOL